The Virtuous Woman in Ruth

Book One
Complete in Christ
A Virtuous Woman Bible Study Series

Deborah Devine

Cover Image:
iStock.com/Kevron2001

DEDICATION

This book is dedicated to my husband, Steven who has always supported and encouraged me in all of my endeavors!

Steven,
You have always set me up for success.
For this I will be forever grateful.
You have lived out the words you so often speak,
"I work so you can work for God."
May the God whom we both serve,
bless you deeply for being such a godly husband.
I love you most!

ACKNOWLEDGMENTS

I must thank my dear friend, Roxann who not only
encouraged me, but served as my grammar editor.
Without her, I would never remember if it's "who" or "whom"!
Thanks #1!

A special thank you to the women in my church women's ministry
group who were willing to be my experimental class, for their support
through both feedback and encouragement.

Thank you to so many other family and friends for their support.

CONTENTS

Preface

I love to share the Word of God! I often do this through my writing. However, like many women today, I find that the business of life repeatedly interferes with my goals. Although I have times where I am able to truly focus on what God has for me; too often life gets in the way. Which is sadly ironic as Christ is the giver of life itself!

Instead of complaining or calling out to God (again) to help me get the entire study ready before sharing, I decided to do what He has laid on my heart to do: find a way to accomplish sharing what God has blessed me with, and help other women take time to be in God's word in a less over-whelming way. So, I split up the contents of the study into shorter, more manageable pieces.

My prayer is that you will receive each book in the series with the original intent: to help uncover what God is asking of women; to break down the misunderstanding of some of the passages in the Bible regarding women; and to uncover some spiritual guidelines He has given us to help us grow.

Above all, my aim is to show the immense love our Lord holds for each of His daughters and for us all to come to a greater appreciation of that love through the study of His word.

Although there are many versions of the Bible available to us today, I will use the New International Version (NIV) during this study unless otherwise stated. I will refer to the King James Version (KJV) in this study from time to time. The language used in the King James Version of the Bible may seem outdated, but I will refer to it mainly because of one word... and that word is "virtuous."

This study is designed to be done either individually or as a group. You can keep it simple, or go into more depth with provided suggestions called *"Digging Deeper."* I hope you take the opportunities given to journal your thoughts (either in this book or in your own personal journal) as well as write out prayers - which you can then use in your prayer time.

I pray this short study book and any others that follow, will bless you in your understanding of God and His Word!

In the Love of Christ,

Deborah

Introduction

Starting the Journey

"Love the Lord your God with all your heart and with all your soul
and with all your mind and with all your strength."
Mark 12:30

Before I started working on this study, my desire was to follow the Lord more closely, so I started asking some basic questions: "What is my part in God's plan? Does He have a destiny for me? What does He expect of me, as a woman? Do I have the same rights as a man? What does God see in me - or essential to my growth - what does He *want* to see in me as His child?"

You too may have found that reading the Bible can often lead to more questions. While God's message of salvation is simple, understanding His word can sometimes be difficult. In finding this the case, I finally submitted to God's prompting and agreed to take time and truly study and meditate on His word. I did so with the hope that He would open my eyes and my heart. He has done that - and more! In fact, He continues to open my eyes, and heart each time I open my Bible. I pray He always will!

Let me admit now, that in no way do I think I have all the answers. I don't believe I ever will. But I do know who does. Once we have identified what we really need answered and understand who our Guide on this journey *must* be, only then can the journey truly begin.

To be honest, I have been filled with more questions, given more things to think about and urged to dig deeper into His word to discover why I was even compelled to ask questions in the first place.

1

What I also learned early on in my studies is that different people have different opinions regarding the questions I was looking to answer. And although we are directed in the Bible to search for wise counsel (*Proverbs 1:5*)[1], I knew I needed to carefully weigh all advice in prayer and against His word. Only through prayer and His word should we draw conclusions as to what the Lord wants of us. If it is not in His word, it is not of His will.

Through this and future studies, I hope to come along side of you for a time on *your* journey and invite you to participate as our Lord unfolds His will for the lives of all women.

We've all been given the same first and most important commandment. A commandment that tells us to, *"Love the Lord your God with all your heart and with all your soul and with all your mind and with all your strength"* Mark 12:30.

This is a difficult goal to accomplish, but not impossible. For this command does not imply perfection as many define the word "perfect," but instead it means *"to be mature"*.

Accomplishing the command given us in *Mark 12:30* involves life changes; growing up, if you will, in Christ. And it most definitely requires the involvement of the Holy Spirit, for it is by *His* strength that we mature, not our own. It is a goal that once reached, will easily escape us; one that we will need to recapture again and again. It is a lifelong journey. A journey the Lord absolutely must and amazingly *wants* to share in. In fact, it was He who initiated that journey in the first place.

1 John 4:19 says, *"We love Him, because He first loved us."* And God will also be the One to complete our journey, *"He who began a good work in you will carry it on to completion until the day of Christ Jesus"* Philippians 1:6.

To become the women God made us to be, we as women *need* to look at what God is saying to us through the Bible. We *need* to ask God how He sees us; not compared to men, not compared to anyone; but how He sees us as His daughters.

---

[1] *A wise man will hear, and will increase learning; and a man of understanding shall attain unto wise counsels:* (KJV)

We also need to get to *know* Him, His character; the character of God.

Psalm 46:10

> *"Be still and know that I am God;"*

The word, "know" used here has such a deeper meaning than just being aware of something. It means to have respect for and an understanding of something. It is an *action* word! God doesn't just want us to know He exists; He wants us to understand *Who He is!*

My journey continues, and I know I am not alone. Neither are you. God is with us, and I am honored to have this opportunity to journey with you for a time.

For Individual Study:

Read *Proverbs 31:10-31* (found on pages 6 & 7)

Think about the woman described here and write down some of the things that you feel are more than should be expected of you.

For Group Study:

If this study is being done in a small group setting, the facilitator can open with the suggestion below, then each section can be reviewed together as often as you meet.

Facilitator:
Read Introduction.
Have someone in your group read *Proverbs 31:10-31* (found on pages 6 & 7), or take turns reading each verse.

Discuss as a group what you think about the woman described here. Have them share some of the things that they feel are more than should be expected of them.

Scripture Reference

Proverbs 31:10-31 New International Version (NIV)

¹⁰ *A wife of noble character who can find? She is worth far more than rubies.* *

¹¹ *Her husband has full confidence in her and lacks nothing of value.*

¹² *She brings him good, not harm, all the days of her life.*

¹³ *She selects wool and flax and works with eager hands.*

¹⁴ *She is like the merchant ships, bringing her food from afar.*

¹⁵ *She gets up while it is still night; she provides food for her family and portions for her female servants.*

¹⁶ *She considers a field and buys it; out of her earnings she plants a vineyard.*

¹⁷ *She sets about her work vigorously; her arms are strong for her tasks.*

¹⁸ *She sees that her trading is profitable, and her lamp does not go out at night.*

¹⁹ *In her hand she holds the distaff and grasps the spindle with her fingers.*

²⁰ *She opens her arms to the poor and extends her hands to the needy.*

²¹ *When it snows, she has no fear for her household; for all of them are clothed in scarlet.*

22 She makes coverings for her bed; she is clothed in fine linen and purple.

23 Her husband is respected at the city gate, where he takes his seat among the elders of the land.

24 She makes linen garments and sells them, and supplies the merchants with sashes.

25 She is clothed with strength and dignity; she can laugh at the days to come.

26 She speaks with wisdom, and faithful instruction is on her tongue.

27 She watches over the affairs of her household and does not eat the bread of idleness.

28 Her children arise and call her blessed; her husband also, and he praises her:

29 "Many women do noble things, but you surpass them all."

30 Charm is deceptive, and beauty is fleeting; but a woman who fears the LORD is to be praised.

31 Honor her for all that her hands have done, and let her works bring her praise at the city gate.

* Proverbs 31:10 King James Version (KJV)

10 Who can find a _virtuous_ woman? for her price is far above rubies.

[emphasis added]

7

Chapter One

Virtuous Woman

Take a moment to settle your heart and mind before you begin. A good way to do this is to pray Scripture. I suggest:

> *Show me your ways, LORD,*
> *teach me your paths.*
> *Guide me in your truth and teach me…*
> *Psalm 25:4-5a*

Start by rereading *Proverbs 31:10-31* found on pages six and seven.

I don't know about you, but it wears me out just reading this! I mean, this woman sounds just too good to be true!

Let's take a moment and look at that unique word, "virtuous", that the King James Version uses to describe this ideal woman.

Words used in other versions of the Bible in place of the word "virtuous" are; "noble, worthy, good" and even "capable". But in my mind, the word "virtuous" stands alone. The dictionary defines "virtuous" as: *"having morality, goodness or uprightness; a special type of goodness."* (1)

It's "a special type *of goodness"* that drew me to the word "virtuous," and even to this passage about a virtuous woman in the first place; as well as the realization that this description of a virtuous woman has confused and intimidated many women throughout history!

The woman described in these passages is so "perfect". She is someone we may admire, but find quite difficult to be like. And when we add in other verses about women found throughout the Bible, it seems outright impossible to be a virtuous woman. You may even think these verses are chauvinistic and outdated - and not just because of the wording, but because of what she represents.

I was so confused about what God expected of me as a woman! I struggled with trying to live a life that was honoring to God, without falling into the clichéd female role of past generations. Yet, when I ignored the scripture and saw these obvious guidelines to be old fashioned, I knew I was dismissing some of God's word and then guilt, as you might expect, would set in.

I was clearly missing something!

What resulted was a constant struggle as I tried over and over again to fix my life. But I was missing the point! I was trying to accomplish on my own what only God can do. *And*, because much of my understanding was being polluted by the interpretation of others, I was left feeling completely inadequate because I did not stand up to her ideal behavior.

I wanted to get all cleaned up first before going to God for help. Have you ever felt that way? (Write your thoughts either below or in your personal journal).

Now, some people do believe the verses found in Proverbs are meant to be taken literally by women; while others claim they don't apply to us today. The obvious problems with these explanations are that they open up either opportunity for the oppression of women or allow us to dismiss a portion of God's teaching. Either way, it is no wonder we end up confused and stuck in our spiritual growth.

The most popular approach used today is that while the description of a virtuous woman may have been appropriate when it was written, it is only the moral principles reflected in these verses that are intended guidelines for all time.

This idea is much more practical. It allows us to pick out basic ideas such as "use your time wisely" and "help the needy," and apply them to everyday living today; while overlooking the obvious cultural differences like "selecting wool and flax." However, such picking and choosing not only allows us "wiggle room" in interpretation, but surely also leads to an incomplete picture.

The goal of this study is to show that we *can* look at this description, and other passages in the Bible about women, in a deeper and more complete way. It *is* possible for us to be virtuous women without sacrificing our personalities, our hopes, and our dreams! In fact, God designed us *all* to be godly women regardless of what we do or how the world may define us.

It *is* true that the guidelines found in this description of a virtuous woman are still an important tool for godly living today. We just have to look at them in the right light. We must not dismiss them as old fashioned, for God's Word exceeds *all* time. Let me use God's own word to explain what I mean.

Revelation 22:13

> *I am the Alpha and the Omega, the First and the Last, the Beginning and the End.*

Now *John 1:1, 1:14*

> *¹ In the beginning was the Word, and the Word was with God, and the Word was God.*
>
> *¹⁴ The Word became flesh* [Jesus] *and made his dwelling among us. We have seen his glory, the glory of the one and only Son, who came from the Father, full of grace and truth.* [my notation]

What can we learn about Jesus in *Revelation 22:13* and *John 1:1?*

Here we learn that Jesus is referred to as the Word, and the Word is eternal. What was written yesterday still holds true today, while giving us hope in tomorrow. The Bible, God's word, is a narrative of God's love in which Jesus is the beginning, throughout history, and will be in the end.

Again, the description of the virtuous woman holds many guidelines for living, and although it is important not to confuse guidelines we find in the Bible with God's commands, we shouldn't take either lightly.

The definition of the word "guideline" is, *"a cord or rope to aid a passer over a difficult point or to permit retracing a course"* and *"an indication or outline of policy or conduct."* [1]

God's word is a like an actual rope that we can hang onto as we walk the difficult road of life. It even allows us to retrace our steps when we get off course, leading us back to the right path, His path. God's word *is* the outline we must follow for right conduct. The Bible is our guideline - Jesus is our Guide! And as we will find when we follow His Guideline, we will automatically keep His commands. When we keep His commands, we can't help but follow The Guide!

Jesus Christ said, *"Do not think that I have come to abolish the Law or the Prophets; I have not come to abolish them but to fulfill them,"* Matthew 5:17.

Sometimes we ignore Christ's fulfillment and do things on our own. We try to become virtuous women through our own actions. This is when we always fail. Christ has called us to be virtuous women. And God never calls us to do something unless He intends to equip us in doing it. We are told just how we are equipped in the very passage that calls us to this action!

2 Peter 1:3 (NIV)

> *His divine power has given us everything we need for a godly life through our knowledge of Him who called us by His own glory and goodness.*

Here's that same passage from the *King James Version* of the Bible. Yes, I know, it is old fashioned language, but humor me:

2 Peter 1:3 (KJV)

> *According as His divine power hath given unto us all things that pertain unto life and godliness, through the knowledge of him that hath called us to glory and <u>virtue</u>.* [emphasis added]

According to the King James version, what are we called to?

And how has God equipped us to do so?

His *divine power* has given us all things that pertain to life and godliness, through the *knowledge* of Him!

The New Testament of the Bible was originally written in Greek. Sometimes looking at the definition of those original Greek words helps us understand the full meaning behind the text.

The Greek word for *knowledge* used in this passage is *"epignosis,"* meaning *"recognition, full discernment, and acknowledgement."* It is a form of the word *"epiginosko,"* which means *"to become fully acquainted with."* [2]

So, in order to become virtuous, we must not end our search for the truth of the passages describing a virtuous woman by simply trying to apply the practical guidelines. We must look deeper; searching for knowledge of Him, so that we may become fully acquainted with the Truth that is Christ.

Throughout the Bible we see verses having a specific meaning while also teaching practical values. However, we often find places where there is a metaphorical or symbolic meaning.

There's another one of those "unique" words I love! A metaphor is an idea or figure of speech that is used to symbolize something else.

Matthew 13:3a

> *Then he told them many things in parables...*

In other words, Jesus used a simple story - or metaphor - to symbolically teach His followers.

In the original Hebrew, the description of a virtuous woman found in *Proverbs 31* is written metaphorically, as an acrostic; that is to say that the first letter of each of the twenty-two verses begins with a consecutive letter of the Hebrew alphabet. Because of this, the passage has been referred to as the ABC's of the perfect wife - *no pressure there!*

Not only do these verses contain successive Hebrew letters, but *all* of the letters in the Hebrew alphabet, in order, from Alef to Tav (i.e. A to Z). It's not just the Hebrew alphabet - but the *complete* Hebrew alphabet.

Well, I love puzzles! And since Jesus Himself often used symbolic puzzles in the form of parables when He taught, I was immediately intrigued by God's use of such a design here! Since all acrostics spell out a word, name or motto (the very definition of acrostic), I couldn't help but ask, "What motto is God sharing with us? Surely, it's more than how to be the perfect wife? Can an unmarried woman be virtuous? What about a widow or a divorced woman? Must a woman spin, sew and garden to be virtuous?"

Matthew 5:48

> *Therefore be perfect, even as your Father who is in heaven is perfect.*

What word is used to describe what our behavior should be?

What word is used to describe our Father in heaven?

A bit intimidating, wouldn't you say?!

In pondering these thoughts, the word *"complete"* kept hitting my heart. The description of a virtuous woman, I realized is not about being perfect.

The description of a Virtuous Woman is about being Complete!

Romans 3:22-24

> *This righteousness is given through faith in Jesus Christ to all who believe. There is no difference between Jew and Gentile, [23] for all have sinned and fall short of the glory of God, [24] and all are justified freely by his grace through the redemption that came by Christ Jesus.*

According to *verse 23*, what have we all done (fill in the blanks)?

"For all have _____ and _____ _____ of the glory of God."

So according to this verse, can we be perfect?

Great news! Christ is not expecting us to be "perfect" in our common understanding of the word: *"having no mistakes or flaws.* [1]

Appropriately, "complete" is the first word used in the definition of *"telios,"* the Greek word for "perfect," as used in *Matthew 5:48*. *Telios* refers to *maturity*, describing a man (or woman) of *completeness: of full age regarding mental and moral character.* [2]

There is only one truly perfect person who has ever walked the Earth: Jesus Christ. And it is only through following Him that we can receive the gift of *His* righteous perfection.

The description of a virtuous woman given us in Proverbs is not about accomplishing perfection as the world understands it. It is not about being a super woman, or the perfect wife. The description shows a woman complete - *complete in Christ.*

Although the description found in Proverbs does lay out in an orderly manner the characteristics needed to be virtuous, it is when we cross-reference these passages with other books and verses in the Bible that the true *spiritual* picture takes form.

Verses ten through thirty-one in *Proverbs chapter 31*, paint a picture that reveals the Truth in our Lord, Jesus Christ. Understanding the image of the woman they create is essential to our growth; our maturity in Christ.

Finish chapter one by writing out *Matthew 5:48* in your own words substituting "complete" for the word "perfect."

Therefore be perfect, even as your Father who is in heaven is perfect.

Digging Deeper

Read *Matthew 6:25-34* aloud.

> *"Therefore I tell you, do not worry about your life, what you will eat or drink; or about your body, what you will wear. Is not life more than food, and the body more than clothes?* [26] *Look at the birds of the air; they do not sow or reap or store away in barns, and yet your heavenly Father feeds them. Are you not much more valuable than they?* [27] *Can any one of you by worrying add a single hour to your life?*

> [28] *"And why do you worry about clothes? See how the flowers of the field grow. They do not labor or spin.* [29] *Yet I tell you that not even Solomon in all his splendor was dressed like one of these.* [30] *If that is how God clothes the grass of the field, which is here today and tomorrow is thrown into the fire, will he not much more clothe you—you of little faith?*

> [31] *So do not worry, saying, 'What shall we eat?' or 'What shall we drink?' or 'What shall we wear?'* [32] *For the pagans run after all these things, and your heavenly Father knows that you need them.* [33] *But seek first his kingdom and his righteousness, and all these things will be given to you as well.*

> [34] *Therefore do not worry about tomorrow, for tomorrow will worry about itself. Each day has enough trouble of its own.*

Think about what it means to *seek first his kingdom and his righteousness.*

Write out a prayer thanking God for His promise that He will provide everything we need, if we will only trust in Him.

.

Chapter Two

Introducing Ruth

Take a moment to settle your heart and mind before you begin.

> *Show me your ways, LORD,*
> *teach me your paths.*
> *Guide me in your truth and teach me...*
> *Psalm 25:4-5a*

Read how a man named Boaz described a woman named Ruth in *Ruth 3:11,* according to the *King James Version* of the Bible.

> *And now, my daughter, fear not; I will do to thee*
> *all that thou requirest: for all the city of my people doth*
> *know that thou art a virtuous woman.*

What word does Boaz use to describe what kind of woman Ruth is?

In fact, the only woman in the Bible to be directly described as "virtuous" is Ruth. What a compliment!

Ruth is the perfect example of a virtuous woman because she is someone to whom we can physically relate. The Lord knows that women like a complete picture - not just a description, but an example to go with it! So, He gave us a real-life example of a virtuous woman in Ruth. A

21

woman who lived in Old Testament times, therefore likely someone who performed the necessary tasks while upholding the principles outlined in *Proverbs*.

What made Ruth virtuous? And, important for inspiration, what was her reward? Let's find out:

Ruth1:1-5

> *In the days when the judges ruled, there was a famine in the land. So a man from Bethlehem in Judah, together with his wife and two sons, went to live for a while in the country of Moab. ²The man's name was Elimelek, his wife's name was Naomi, and the names of his two sons were Mahlon and Kilion. They were Ephrathites from Bethlehem, Judah. And they went to Moab and lived there.*
> *³Now Elimelek, Naomi's husband, died, and she was left with her two sons. ⁴They married Moabite women, one named Orpah and the other Ruth. After they had lived there about ten years, ⁵both Mahlon and Kilion also died, and Naomi was left without her two sons and her husband.*

The book of Ruth starts out by setting the scene for the story of the relationship between Ruth and Naomi. Within the first five verses of the book of Ruth, all the men in this family have died. We really don't learn anything about them. They are basically used to introduce the women. Now the story of Ruth and Naomi's relationship can begin.

Ruth1:6-7

> *When Naomi heard in Moab that the LORD had come to the aid of his people by providing food for them, she and her daughters-in-law prepared to return home from there. ⁷With her two daughters-in-law she left the place where she had been living and set out on the road that would take them back to the land of Judah.*

According to these verses, what does Naomi learn that makes her decide to return home to Judah?

When Naomi and her two daughters-in-law (Ruth and Orpah) get to the main road, Naomi tells the girls that instead of going on with her to Bethlehem, they should remain in Moab and return to their own families. When they protest, Naomi breaks into a long lecture about how she has nothing left to offer them.

Ruth 1:11-13

> *But Naomi said, "Return home, my daughters. Why would you come with me? Am I going to have any more sons, who could become your husbands?* [12] *Return home, my daughters; I am too old to have another husband. Even if I thought there was still hope for me— even if I had a husband tonight and then gave birth to sons—* [13] *would you wait until they grew up? Would you remain unmarried for them? No, my daughters. It is more bitter for me than for you, because the LORD's hand has turned against me!"*

From these verses, do you think Naomi has stopped believing in God? (Explain your answer):

Naomi still accepts God's existence, but she clearly isn't trusting in Him. In fact, she is choosing to believe that His hand has gone out against her (*vs.13*).

23

Take a moment to reflect on a time when you were tempted to feel that God's hand had gone out against you. (Write your thoughts either below or in your personal journal).

Naomi is having a real spiritual breakdown here, and for very good reason; not only had she lost her husband, but now she's lost both sons!

I have found it can be extremely difficult trying to support someone in such a depressed state. Although I want to be there for them, I often can't help but think that it would be so much easier to just walk away, to take the easy road and just go home. Orpah did just that, she simply kissed her mother-in-law good-bye and went home.

Ruth 1:14-15

> *At this they wept aloud again. Then Orpah kissed her mother-in-law goodbye, but Ruth clung to her.*
> *15 "Look," said Naomi, "your sister-in-law is going back to her people and her gods. Go back with her."*

If the story is about Ruth, why do you think we need to know about Naomi's other daughter-in-law's choice?

Orpah provides the contrast we need to fully understand Ruth's commitment. In Orpah's decision, I was able to see the many times in my own life when I had decided on the easier road. Sometimes people and/or circumstances can be so overwhelming, we just don't know how to handle them. We sometimes make decisions based on what we think we can handle, rather than what God will equip us to handle.

God once had me placed near a friend who was suffering from alcoholism. I was free to come and go in her life, but I chose to remain available to her. After much work on her part, she overcame her addiction and was on the road to recovery. The words she spoke to me at that time will stay with me forever. She said, "you told me you would come back, and you did." Little did I know that by not turning my back on her, I would help her have the strength to fight.

Now, it is *extremely important* for me to note here that I am not talking about staying in a relationship that is destructive and harmful. Occasionally God has us in a position to help another, *but never at the cost of our own safety and well-being!* Sometimes our only choice is to walk away! Staying in an abusive relationship will only allow the cycle to continue, and that helps no-one.

Orpah's decision to leave Ruth and Naomi was *not* based on her safety, but on her own comfort. I am still learning how not to pick and choose what road I think God wants me to go down based on what is more comfortable for me. Sometimes walking away from a destructive relationship and toward God is harder and more uncomfortable than staying. Such was the case with me in leaving the known patterns of an abusive husband, with two kids to care for, and walking into the unknown.

God doesn't expect us to carry every burden, but He does expect us to listen to His Spirit telling us which ones we should. And He never asks us to do it alone!

What is most convicting to me in this part of the story is the emphasis that when Orpah turns away, she is not only returning to her family and her people, but to *her gods*. Ouch. What a harsh truth it was to learn that when I turn *away* from God, I inevitably turn *toward* something else, and often that something becomes *my god!*

What is it that you often turn to when you are in need of comfort from the stresses of life (for example: food, drugs or alcohol, television, exercise or sleep)?

Some of these things, in moderation are not necessarily bad. So, how can we enjoy such activities without letting them replace God in our lives? (Write your thoughts either below or in your personal journal).

Finally, we have Ruth's reaction. She clings to Naomi. Ruth doesn't just bite her lip and say, "No, that's okay, I'll stay with you" in a halfhearted manner. She clings to her! Where words have failed, Ruth turns to action! When Naomi urges her to go with Orpah, Ruth in essence, says "NO!" And here begins a wonderful depiction of Ruth's great love for Naomi.

Ruth 1:16-17

> *But Ruth replied, "Don't urge me to leave you or to turn back from you. Where you go I will go, and where you stay I will stay. Your people will be my people and your God my God. ¹⁷ Where you die I will die, and there I will be buried. May the LORD deal with me, be it ever so severely, if anything but death separates you and me."*

What devotion! Ruth chooses a whole new life with Naomi. She chooses a new home, new land, new people - *and* more importantly,

Ruth chooses God.

Does Ruth inspire you to renew your reliance on God in any areas in your life? If so, how? (Write your thoughts either below or in your personal journal).

Ruth 1:18-19

> When Naomi realized that Ruth was determined to go with her, she stopped urging her.
> ¹⁹ So the two women went on until they came to Bethlehem. When they arrived in Bethlehem, the whole town was stirred because of them, and the women exclaimed, "Can this be Naomi?"

The verses that follow tell us, when Naomi realizes Ruth is determined to go with her, she stops asking her to leave; but as we read on, she doesn't appear to be very grateful.

Scripture offers additional comparison here, this time between Ruth and Naomi. Where Ruth turns to God for comfort, Naomi blames Him for her pain.

Notice what happens when the women get to Bethlehem. The people of the town are moved to see Naomi, they even call out her name which... *she promptly changes!*

Ruth 1:20-21

> *"Don't call me Naomi," she told them. "Call me Mara, because the Almighty has made my life very bitter. ²¹ I went away full, but the LORD has brought me back empty. Why call me Naomi? The LORD has afflicted me; the Almighty has brought misfortune upon me."*

What do you think the name *Mara* means?

As you probably guessed, *Mara* means *bitter!* And what's with Naomi claiming she went away full and came home empty? What about Ruth? Naomi doesn't say, "but my daughter-in-law has stayed by my side!" or "but if it hadn't been for Ruth…" No. Naomi just persists with an attitude of despair. Yet, Ruth stays by Naomi's side and continues to care for her. And remember, Ruth was mourning the loss of her own husband, as well!

Have you ever experienced a time when you knew you had to stick with something even though you did not feel like it, because you knew it was for the best? What did you do to carry on in that situation? (Write your thoughts below or in your personal journal).

Hebrews 12:1

> *Therefore, since we are surrounded by such a great*
> *cloud of witnesses, let us throw off everything that hinders*
> *and the sin that so easily entangles, and let us run with*
> *perseverance the race marked out for us.*

Do you think that her perseverance and commitment to Naomi affected what people thought of Ruth? Let's jump ahead in the story to the moment Ruth meets Boaz.

Ruth 2:10-11

> *At this, she bowed down with her face to the*
> *ground. She asked him, "Why have I found such favor*
> *in your eyes that you notice me—a foreigner?"*
> *11 Boaz replied, "I've been told all about what you*
> *have done for your mother-in-law since the death of your*
> *husband—how you left your father and mother and your*
> *homeland and came to live with a people you did not*
> *know before."*

I think from this passage showing how people were inspired by Ruth's commitment to Naomi, the answer to the above question is, "Yes, definitely!"

Finish chapter two by reading *Hebrews 10:36* aloud.

> *You need to persevere so that when you have done*
> *the will of God, you will receive what he has promised.*

Write out a prayer to God for strength and perseverance, to know and do His will, that He may bless you with His promises.

Digging Deeper

Read *Hebrews 12:1-3* aloud.

> *Therefore, since we are surrounded by such a great cloud of witnesses, let us throw off everything that hinders and the sin that so easily entangles. And let us run with perseverance the race marked out for us, ²fixing our eyes on Jesus, the pioneer and perfecter of faith. For the joy set before him he endured the cross, scorning its shame, and sat down at the right hand of the throne of God. ³Consider him who endured such opposition from sinners, so that you will not grow weary and lose heart.*

Reflect and pray about what may be hindering and entangling you in your faith walk. How can you throw those things off and fix your eyes on Jesus?

Chapter Three

Actions and Reward

Take a moment to settle your heart and mind before you begin.

> *Show me your ways, LORD,*
> *teach me your paths.*
> *Guide me in your truth and teach me…*
> *Psalm 25:4-5a*

Review the scripture we started with in chapter two by rereading the *KJV* of *Ruth 3:11,*

> *"And now, my daughter, fear not; I will do to thee*
> *all that thou requirest: for all the city of my people doth*
> *know that thou art a virtuous woman."*

We already know that Ruth is considered a virtuous woman. The Bible tells us directly through this statement by Boaz. Her actions toward her mother-in-law were certainly praiseworthy, but were they the *only* reason she was considered virtuous? (Explain your answer).

We can probably conclude that Ruth lived up to her culture's desirable qualities as described in *Proverbs'* description of a virtuous woman. Even so, let's look at the basic values being taught in *Proverbs*, and see how Ruth stacks up. To do this comparison, we will go back and forth from *Ruth* to *Proverbs*.

Proverbs 31:10

> *Who can find a virtuous woman? for her price is far above rubies.* (KJV)

Circle all words that apply to a virtuous woman.

Valuable   Common   Rare   Worthless   Imaginary

A virtuous woman is hard to find; she is rare and valuable: Ruth is a rare woman. Remember, she is the only woman in the Bible to be described as virtuous. And frankly, not many women would give up the opportunity to go home to Mom and Dad after losing their husband; rather than following their mother-in-law to a strange country.

Orpah didn't, but Ruth did just that. And she did so unselfishly; with compassion, strength and a great love.

Proverbs 31:27

> *She watches over the affairs of her household and does not eat the bread of idleness.*

What kind of bread does a virtuous woman not eat?

So, a virtuous woman is willing to work, is not lazy and uses her time wisely: All things I think we can attribute to Ruth quite easily.

Ruth 2:2-7

> *And Ruth the Moabite said to Naomi, "Let me go to the fields and pick up the leftover grain behind anyone in whose eyes I find favor."*
>
> *Naomi said to her, "Go ahead, my daughter." ³So she went out, entered a field and began to glean behind the harvesters. As it turned out, she was working in a field belonging to Boaz, who was from the clan of Elimelek.*
>
> [remember Naomi and her husband were from this family line as well]
>
> *⁴Just then Boaz arrived from Bethlehem and greeted the harvesters, "The LORD be with you!"*
>
> *"The LORD bless you!" they answered.*
>
> *⁵Boaz asked the overseer of his harvesters, "Who does that young woman belong to?"*
>
> *⁶The overseer replied, "She is the Moabite who came back from Moab with Naomi. ⁷She said, 'Please let me glean and gather among the sheaves behind the harvesters.' She came into the field and has remained here from morning till now, except for a short rest in the shelter."* [my notation]

Ruth shows eagerness to go out and provide for herself and Naomi upon their arrival in Bethlehem. She, herself suggests that she go behind the harvesters and pick up the leftovers, as was common practice in those days. And then she works steadily with only a short rest.

Now back to the description of a virtuous woman.

Proverbs 31:26

> *She speaks with wisdom,*
> *and faithful instruction is on her tongue.*

The description of a virtuous woman says she speaks with wisdom, tactfulness, and kindness. Throughout the story, we see Ruth as being quite wise in her humble behavior toward the Israelites. She asks politely before gathering behind the harvesters (seen in *Ruth 2:7* above).

And Ruth is genuinely thankful for Boaz' support and protection when she asks;

Ruth 2:13:

> *"May I continue to find favor in your eyes, my lord, you have put me at ease by speaking kindly to your servant—though I do not have the standing of one of your servants."*

Proverbs 31:20

> *She* [a virtuous woman] *opens her arms to the poor and extends her hands to the needy.* [my notation]

To whom does a virtuous woman open her arms and extend her hands? (Circle all that apply).

Wealthy   Poor   Needy   Israelites   Moabites

The virtuous woman aids the needy and the poor: We already know Ruth has upheld this principle: she came to the aide of Naomi.

Reread Boaz' words to Ruth in *Ruth 2:11,*

> *Boaz replied, "I've been told all about what you have done for your mother-in-law since the death of your husband—how you left your father and mother and your homeland and came to live with a people you did not know before.*

Ruth had chosen to aide Naomi and in doing so, she was aiding a widow in her time of need.

Finally, *Proverbs 31:11-12, 23 & 28*

> *Her husband has full confidence in her*
> *and lacks nothing of value.*
> *¹²She brings him good, not harm,*
> *all the days of her life.*

> *²³Her husband is respected at the city gate, where he*
> *takes his seat among the elders of the land.*
> *²⁸Her children arise and call her blessed;*
> *her husband also, and he praises her.*

In these verses we find a virtuous woman is a treasure to her husband. He knows she is trustworthy. She is good to her husband, and her husband is known and respected because of it, and...

Hold on! Wait a minute – Ruth is a widow!

It is *very important* that we make this connection! At this point in the story, Ruth's husband is deceased and she has yet to marry Boaz! (Spoiler Alert!) It is when Boaz first meets her that he calls her "virtuous." He did not know her when her husband was alive - nor did anyone in Bethlehem. She did not live in Bethlehem until after her husband's death.

If Ruth had been referred to as virtuous *after* she had re-married, one might assume that her being virtuous had something to do with her status as the wife of Boaz. But Boaz and his people recognize Ruth as being a virtuous woman while she is at her *lowest* status.

Ruth is a widow, therefore no longer pure. She is a foreigner in their country, a stranger to their people. This point is emphasized *six times* throughout the book of *Ruth*. But Boaz says that all his people know that Ruth is a virtuous woman. So, it is clear that Boaz and his people knew Ruth as virtuous by her actions toward Naomi, her mother-in-law. But... *was* it simply her actions toward Naomi? (Write your thoughts below).

As we have already learned, Boaz says when he first meets Ruth:

Ruth 2:11

> *"I've been told all about what you have done for
> your mother-in-law since the death of your husband -
> how you left your father and mother and your homeland
> and came to live with a people you did not know before."*

So surely, character and integrity *are* playing a hand here. But let's look further at what Boaz had to say about Ruth's virtue.

Ruth 2:12

> May the LORD repay you for what you have done.
> May you be richly rewarded by the LORD, the God of
> Israel, under whose wings you have come to take refuge."

This is very significant. Whose wings did Boaz say Ruth had taken refuge under?

This says so much about why Ruth is considered virtuous!

We need to give credit where credit is due here. God had *everything* to do with Ruth being described as a virtuous woman! Her actions toward her mother-in-law, though heroic and certainly praiseworthy, were far less important than her *trust in God.*

Proverbs 31:29-31

> *"Many women do noble things,
> but you surpass them all."*
> *30 Charm is deceptive, and beauty is fleeting; but a
> woman who fears* [stands in awe of] *the LORD is to be
> praised. 31 Honor her for all that her hands have done,
> and let her works bring her praise at the city gate.*

[my notation]

Through this verse and Ruth as an example, I have learned that any one of us may be a wonderfully compassionate and unselfish person, a great candidate for being a virtuous woman; but it is <u>GOD</u> who completes that transformation in us.

Therefore, whether a wife, a widow, a single or divorced woman; although all provide opportunity to be virtuous, our marital status is not what makes us a virtuous woman.

God does that!

Proverbs 31:23 again,

> *Her husband is respected at the city gate, where he takes his seat among the elders of the land.*

Now let's see if once Ruth marries Boaz, she fulfills this description.

Ruth 4:11

> *Then the elders and all the people at the gate said, "We are witnesses. May the LORD make the woman who is coming into your home* [Ruth] *like Rachel and Leah, who together built up the family of Israel. May you have standing in Ephrathah and be famous in Bethlehem.* [my notation]

What do the elders and all those at the gate call themselves?

Let's go to the end of the description of a virtuous woman.

Proverbs 31:31

> *Honor her for all that her hands have done, and let her works bring her praise at the city gate.*

Just so we can conquer any question left as to whether or not God bestowed upon Ruth the title of a virtuous woman, let's see what He gave her as her reward.

Ruth 4:13-17

> *So Boaz took Ruth and she became his wife. When he made love to her, the LORD enabled her to conceive, and she gave birth to a son.* ¹⁴ *The women said to Naomi: "Praise be to the LORD, who this day has not left you without a guardian-redeemer. May he become famous throughout Israel!* ¹⁵ *He will renew your life and sustain you in your old age. For your daughter-in-law, who loves you and who is better to you than seven sons, has given him birth."*
>
> ¹⁶ *Then Naomi took the child in her arms and cared for him.* ¹⁷ *The women living there said, "Naomi has a son!" And they named him Obed. He was the father of Jesse, the father of David.*

The lineage spoken of here is of great significance. Let's explore. To do this we will go to the New Testament and read *Acts 13:22.*

> *After removing Saul, he made David their king. God testified concerning him: 'I have found David son of Jesse, a man after my own heart; he will do everything I want him to do.'*

Put a number next to the name in the order of their lineage.

____ Jesse

____ Obed

____ David

____ Ruth (Boaz)

Ruth gave birth to Obed. Obed fathered Jesse who in turn fathered David.

To connect the genealogy further, first read *Matthew 1:5-16.*

> *Salmon the father of Boaz, whose mother was Rahab,*
> **Boaz the father of Obed, whose mother was Ruth,**
> **Obed the father of Jesse,**
> **⁶ and Jesse the father of King David.**
> *David was the father of Solomon, whose mother had been Uriah's wife,*
> *⁷ Solomon the father of Rehoboam,*
> *Rehoboam the father of Abijah,*
> *Abijah the father of Asa,*
> *⁸ Asa the father of Jehoshaphat,*
> *Jehoshaphat the father of Jehoram,*
> *Jehoram the father of Uzziah,*
> *⁹ Uzziah the father of Jotham,*
> *Jotham the father of Ahaz,*
> *Ahaz the father of Hezekiah,*
> *¹⁰ Hezekiah the father of Manasseh,*
> *Manasseh the father of Amon,*
> *Amon the father of Josiah,*
> *¹¹ and Josiah the father of Jeconiah and his brothers at the time of the exile to Babylon.*
> *¹² After the exile to Babylon:*
> *Jeconiah was the father of Shealtiel,*
> *Shealtiel the father of Zerubbabel,*
> *¹³ Zerubbabel the father of Abihud,*
> *Abihud the father of Eliakim,*
> *Eliakim the father of Azor,*
> *¹⁴ Azor the father of Zadok,*
> *Zadok the father of Akim,*
> *Akim the father of Elihud,*
> *¹⁵ Elihud the father of Eleazar,*
> *Eleazar the father of Matthan,*
> *Matthan the father of Jacob,*
> *¹⁶ and Jacob the father of* **Joseph, the husband of Mary, and Mary was the mother of Jesus who is called the Messiah.**
> [emphasis added]

39

With whom does this lineage end?

Next *Isaiah 11:1-3a*

> *A shoot will come up from the stump of Jesse; from*
> *his roots a Branch will bear fruit.*
> *² The Spirit of the LORD will rest on him—*
> *the Spirit of wisdom and of understanding,*
> *the Spirit of counsel and of might,*
> *the Spirit of the knowledge and fear of the LORD—*
> *³ and he will delight in the fear of the LORD.*

Who will rest on this Branch from Jesse's roots?

Now *Matthew 3:16-17* and *John 1:32-34*

> *¹⁶ As soon as Jesus was baptized, he went up out of*
> *the water. At that moment heaven was opened, and he*
> *saw the Spirit of God descending like a dove and*
> *alighting on him. ¹⁷ And a voice from heaven said, "This*
> *is my Son, whom I love; with him I am well pleased."*
>
> *³² Then John gave this testimony: "I saw the Spirit*
> *come down from heaven as a dove and remain on*
> *him. ³³ And I myself did not know him, but the one who*
> *sent me to baptize with water told me, 'The man on*
> *whom you see the Spirit come down and remain is the*
> *one who will baptize with the Holy Spirit.' ³⁴ I have seen*
> *and I testify that this is God's Chosen One."*

According to *Matthew* and *John*, who is the one being referred to in the *Book of Isaiah*?

That Branch that bore fruit from the root of Jesse
was none other than our LORD, JESUS CHRIST!

What an honor! Ruth gave birth to a son who the woman of Bethlehem proclaimed should become *"famous throughout Israel!"* A son who they said would renew Naomi's life and sustain her in her old age (*Ruth 4:14-15*). Ruth gave birth to a son who would be counted among the lineage of Jesus Christ Himself!

Acts 13:23

> *From this man's* [David's] *descendants God has brought to Israel the Savior Jesus, as he promised.*
> [my notation]

So much for Naomi coming home empty!

Finish chapter three by reading *John 3:16* aloud.

> *For God so loved the world that he gave his one and only Son, that whoever believes in him shall not perish but have eternal life.*

Write out a pray to our Lord asking Him for a deeper understanding of what it means to truly believe and trust in Him.

Digging Deeper

Read *James 2:14-17, 21-24* aloud.

> *What good is it, my brothers and sisters, if someone claims to have faith but has no deeds? Can such faith save them? [15] Suppose a brother or a sister is without clothes and daily food. [16] If one of you says to them, "Go in peace; keep warm and well fed," but does nothing about their physical needs, what good is it? [17] In the same way, faith by itself, if it is not accompanied by action, is dead.*
>
> *Was not our father Abraham considered righteous for what he did when he offered his son Isaac on the altar? [22] You see that his faith and his actions were working together, and his faith was made complete by what he did. [23] And the scripture was fulfilled that says, "Abraham believed God, and it was credited to him as righteousness," and he was called God's friend. [24] You see that a person is considered righteous by what they do and not by faith alone.*

Ask the Lord for His guidance as to how to show your faith through action, so that your faith will be made complete.

Chapter Four

Metaphorically Speaking

Take a moment to settle your heart and mind before you begin.

Show me your ways, LORD,
teach me your paths.
Guide me in your truth and teach me...
                                    Psalm 25:4-5a

God points to Ruth as an example of a virtuous woman, whether we look at the description in *Proverbs* from a physical or a metaphorical (symbolic) point of view.

Proverbs 31:10

> *Who can find a virtuous woman? for her price is far above*
> *rubies.* (KJV)

As we have discovered, a woman's trust in God is the key to her being virtuous. So, if a virtuous woman cannot be found among a particular people, could that show a lack of trust in God, with those people? (Explain your answer).

To answer this question, we need to skip back to the very beginning of the Book of *Ruth*.

Now that we know a bit about the characters in this book, read *Ruth 1:1* again:

> *In the days when the judges ruled, there was a famine in the land. So, a man from Bethlehem in Judah, together with his wife and two sons, went to live for a while in the country of Moab.*

Why did Naomi and Elimelech leave Bethlehem in Judah and go to live in Moab?

Why do we need to know specifically that it was a famine that caused Naomi and Elimelech to leave Bethlehem? It may seem simply practical to give a reason, but I have often found that simple words can have great meaning in Scripture.

For most people, the word "famine" will bring to mind a lack of food. And you would be correct if you assumed that this verse is referring to a lack of food, since we have already learned that from *Ruth 1:6;*

> *When Naomi heard in Moab that the* LORD *had come to the aid of his people by providing food for them, she and her daughters-in-law prepared to return home from there.*

However, I do not want to overlook an important connection.

Amos 8:11

> *"The days are coming," declares the Sovereign* LORD, *"when I will send a famine through the land—not a famine of food or a thirst for water, but a famine of hearing the words of the* LORD.

What does *this* particular famine refer to a lack of? (Circle all that apply).

Water   Shelter   Peace   Hearing God's Word   Bread

The only thing referred to in this verse is a lack of hearing God's Word. However, if you also chose peace, I would have to agree with you! Famine during Old Testament times could - and often did - mean a lack of God's direction. No prophets provided by God, no-one to look to for guidance - only silence; a famine from His Word.

Now, I want to clarify that although there are regions of the world today that lack food, it does not mean God is causing famine to happen. We live in a broken world and we suffer because of sin, but wherever there is a follower of Christ – God is with them! His presence may have come and gone in the days of the Old Testament, but because of Christ's promise and by His sacrifice, the Holy Spirit now dwells in those who trust in Him and will never leave! Unfortunately, we can *feel* like God has left us at times, but it is always us who pull away from Him!

Even so, in the Old Testament, when God's people would stop worshipping and trusting in Him, *only then* would God turn away from them and they would find themselves destitute and wanting; they would be in a *spiritual famine*. For example, when Moses was stepping down as leader right before the Israelites were to go into the Promised Land, God stated to Moses that the Israelites would once again turn from Him.

We learn about this in *Deuteronomy 31:16-17.*

> *And the LORD said to Moses: "You are going to rest with your ancestors, and these people will soon prostitute themselves to the foreign gods of the land they are entering. They will forsake me and break the covenant I made with them. [17] And in that day I will become angry with them and forsake them; I will hide my face from them, and they will be destroyed. Many disasters and calamities will come on them, and in*

*that day they will ask, 'Have not these disasters come on
us because our God is not with us?'*

According to *vs. 17*, what does God tell us the people would say is
the reason for the disasters and difficulties they would be enduring?

So, what might have caused the famine Bethlehem was going
through at the time Naomi and her husband left? (See vs.16).

Now remember, we are told that the story of Ruth takes place during
the time of *Judges* in *Ruth 1:1*. This is the very time God had foretold to
Moses in *Deuteronomy!* The last verse in *Judges*, the book previous to the
book of *Ruth*, says it all!

Judges 21:25

> *In those days Israel had no king; everyone did as they
> saw fit.*

What does this verse say Israel lacked? (Circle one).

Judges   Soldiers   King   Temple   Oasis

So, without the guidance of a king, what did the people do?

Wow! Although the Israelites in the land of Judah *were* experiencing
a food famine, they were surely also in a spiritual famine! Their lack of
obedience had likely caused both.

Don't be offended by the language used here. Since God associates our relationship to Him as a marriage, He often refers to us as adulterers, prostitutes and the like. What is being expressed is our tendency as humans to constantly look to other things (idols or gods) to provide what only God, our Creator and Husband can provide. In fact, there is a whole book in the Bible, the Book of *Hosea* that beautifully depicts this dilemma.

Like I mentioned, we will face challenges and suffer hardships in this life as a result of the broken world we live in; but sometimes those challenges and hardships are brought on by none other than ourselves. We often find ourselves in painful places, through lack of obedience and our need to be in control.

Finish chapter four by reading and praying *Psalm 139:23-24* aloud.

Search me, God, and know my heart;
test me and know my anxious thoughts.
24 See if there is any offensive way in me,
and lead me in the way everlasting.

Take some time to listen to God. Remember, we do not hear God with our ears, but with our heart. (Write your thoughts either below or in your personal journal).

Digging Deeper

Read *Hebrews 12:5-11* aloud.

> *And have you completely forgotten this word of encouragement that addresses you as a father addresses his son? It says,*
> *"My son, do not make light of the Lord's discipline, and do not lose heart when he rebukes you,*
> *⁶ because the Lord disciplines the one he loves, and he chastens everyone he accepts as his son."*
>
> *⁷ Endure hardship as discipline; God is treating you as his children. For what children are not disciplined by their father? ⁸ If you are not disciplined—and everyone undergoes discipline—then you are not legitimate, not true sons and daughters at all. ⁹ Moreover, we have all had human fathers who disciplined us and we respected them for it. How much more should we submit to the Father of spirits and live! ¹⁰ They disciplined us for a little while as they thought best; but God disciplines us for our good, in order that we may share in his holiness. ¹¹ No discipline seems pleasant at the time, but painful. Later on, however, it produces a harvest of righteousness and peace for those who have been trained by it.*

Ask the Lord to make it clear to you when struggles are not merely results of living in this broken world, but are the conviction of the Holy Spirit attempting to make you aware of an idol (a harmful habit, thought or belief) in your life.

Chapter Five

Spiritual Famine

Take a moment to settle your heart and mind before you begin.

Show me your ways, LORD,
teach me your paths.
Guide me in your truth and teach me...
                    Psalm 25:4-5a

On day three we looked at Ruth as a stranger in the land of Judah, and we briefly touched on the common practice of going behind the harvesters to pick up the leftovers.

Leviticus 19:9-10

> *"When you reap the harvest of your land, do not reap to the very edges of your field or gather the gleanings* [leftovers] *of your harvest. ¹⁰ Do not go over your vineyard a second time or pick up the grapes that have fallen. Leave them for the poor and the foreigner. I am the LORD your God."* [my notation]

For whom is it that the edge of the fields and the harvest leftovers are to be left untouched?

In these passages we see it's true that God's law for the Israelite's included allowing for the care of the poor and the foreigner by stating that a portion of the fields were to be left unharvested so they may reap from them - and Ruth was definitely a foreigner! She was a Moabitess - a stranger in their country. But if the law allowed for her to gather from the fields, why then was she in danger?

Ruth 2:8-9 and *Ruth 2:22*

> So Boaz said to Ruth, "My daughter, listen to me. Don't go and glean in another field and don't go away from here. Stay here with the women who work for me. ⁹ Watch the field where the men are harvesting, and follow along after the women. I have told the men not to lay a hand on you. And whenever you are thirsty, go and get a drink from the water jars the men have filled."
>
> ²² Naomi said to Ruth her daughter-in-law, "It will be good for you, my daughter, to go with the women who work for him, because in someone else's field you might be harmed."

Why do you suppose that Boaz and Naomi had such concern over Ruth's well-being?

Like me, your first reaction might have been, "because she was not only a foreigner, but also a woman," and you may very well be correct!

Underline who God is protecting with His command in *Exodus 22:21-23*

> "Do not mistreat or oppress a foreigner, for you were foreigners in Egypt.
> ²² "Do not take advantage of the widow or the fatherless.
> ²³ If you do and they cry out to me, I will certainly hear their cry."

Do you think the Israelites in Bethlehem knew this as one of the laws of God, written out by the hand of Moses?

Would you agree then that Ruth's endangerment therefore had something to do with the fact that in that day, *"every man did that which was right in his own eyes" (Judges 21:25b)* (KJV)? (Explain your answer).

This does not mean a lack in their *belief* in God's existence, but it sure speaks volumes as to their *obedience* to God. Remember, Naomi didn't stop believing in God. She stopped trusting in and drawing her strength from Him.

We can believe God exists *and* claim Christ as our Savior, yet still experience emptiness and lack of peace because believing isn't just a state of mind. True belief requires obedience *and* action.

2 Peter 1:3

> *His divine power has given us everything we need for a godly life through our knowledge of him who called us by his own glory and goodness.*

Recall in chapter one how we learned about being called to glory and virtue through the knowledge of Christ. What did we learn was the definition of the original Greek word for "knowledge" used in this verse (see chapter one if needed)?

Being a follower of Christ is about relationship; becoming *"fully acquainted with"* our Lord. Just as when we are disobedient to Him, neglecting our relationship with our Lord God and Savior (which is a form of disobedience), will also bring about spiritual famine.

Now, this is not to say that we one day just reach a point where we suddenly have enough faith. Relationships are built, and trust and love grow; which means they can also be misplaced and neglected – at least on our part.

It is important to know and trust God's promise that He will never leave or forsake us for *at least* two reasons. One, that we recognize when we are pulling away from Him and two, that when He is silent - which does happen - it is not because He has left us, but that He is teaching us something through His silence. In these moments, continue to press into Him and know that He is there!

Have you ever experienced spiritual famine? Can you think of something you may have been doing or not doing that would have accounted for this?

Take a moment to reflect on a time in your walk with Christ when you experienced spiritual famine. If that time is now, pray to the Lord for the Holy Spirit to reveal to you what you need to do to feel His presence for the first time or once again. And remember, because of Jesus' sacrifice, God does not distance Himself from us – it is we who distance ourselves from Him! (Write your thoughts either below or in your personal journal).

Personally, when I stop going to God in prayer, reading His Word and listening to the prompting of the Spirit; when I fill my days with everything but Him, drawing from the world what I think will enrich my life, I end up spiritually starved. Remember Orpah and her gods? It is at times like this that my faith is at its weakest, and I suffer because of it.

Surely their lack of trust in God and turning to other gods caused the Israelites' suffering too. God described it to Moses as *"whoring after the gods of the strangers of the land"* (*Deuteronomy 31:16*) (KJV).

No wonder a virtuous woman was so hard to find!

Finally, another way God uses Ruth as a symbolic example of a virtuous woman is whom she represents. Because the book of *Proverbs* is in the Old Testament, some would have a tendency to associate the "virtuous woman" with an Israelite woman. What nationality was Ruth (Circle one)?

Israelite   Egyptian   Moabite   Ephrathite

Ruth was a Moabitess. She was not of the tribe of Israel, but a foreigner who had chosen to follow the God of Israel despite her nationality. Ruth therefore represents a Gentile. It was by her *faith*, not her *lineage* that she claimed the birthright promises of God.

Romans 10:4, 9-13

> *[4] Christ is the culmination of the law so that there may be righteousness for everyone who believes.*
>
> *[9] If you declare with your mouth, "Jesus is Lord," and believe in your heart that God raised him from the dead, you will be saved. [10] For it is with your heart that you believe and are justified, and it is with your mouth that you profess your faith and are saved. [11] As Scripture says, "Anyone who believes in him will never be put to shame." [12] For there is no difference between Jew and Gentile—the same Lord is Lord of all*

and richly blesses all who call on him, [13] for, "Everyone who calls on the name of the Lord will be saved."

What great news! Anyone can stake claim to His promises. We must only believe, have faith and trust in Jesus.

Romans 10:9 again,

> *If you declare with your mouth, "Jesus is Lord," and believe in your heart that God raised him from the dead, you will be saved.*

If you have never *declared with your mouth that "Jesus is Lord,"* but you want to, please know there are no magic words you must say. Remember, Ruth didn't even pray. She simply told *Naomi* that she was putting her trust in God and lived that trust out in her life!

Salvation is all about our hearts.

Your heavenly Father loves you and wants you to know Him and trust in Him. And Jesus gave His life to make sure that was possible. It's that simple.

If you are ready, take a moment to thank God for the sacrifice of His Son, Jesus. Ask forgiveness for your sins, for the Holy Spirit to dwell in your heart to guide you and know in your heart that He loves you and wants a relationship with you.

Again, do not worry about your words, God knows your heart, but please contact the facilitator of this study or a trusted Christian friend to help you in your next steps!

Welcome to God's family!

Finish chapter five by reading *Mark 12:30* aloud.

> *Love the Lord your God with all your heart and with all your soul and with all your mind and with all your strength.*

Pray to the Lord for a deeper understanding of what it means to love Him in all these different ways (heart, mind, body and spirit).

Digging Deeper

Read *Romans 8:14-16* aloud.

> *For those who are led by the Spirit of God are the children of God.[15] The Spirit you received does not make you slaves, so that you live in fear again; rather, the Spirit you received brought about your adoption to sonship* [daughter-ship]. *And by him we cry, "Abba, Father." [16] The Spirit himself testifies with our spirit that we are God's children.* [my addition]

Meditate on what it means to have been given this Spirit of daughter-ship allowing us to claim the birthright promises of God.

Write a prayer to God below, thanking Him for His Spirit.

Chapter Six

Kinsman Redeemer

Take a moment to settle your heart and mind and, if you are ready, pray for guidance from the Holy Spirit before you begin. If you need help, a suggested prayer would be:

"Oh, Holy Spirit, my comforter and counselor, make clear to me what the Lord wants me to learn from His word today."
You can follow this with,

> *Show me your ways, LORD,*
> *teach me your paths.*
> *Guide me in your truth and teach me...*
> *Psalm 25:4-5a*

We have learned that a woman being virtuous has everything to do with her trust in God. However, in order for a woman to *trust* in God, she must first *recognize* Him. It is again in the book of Ruth where we find our real-life example:

Ruth 1:16

> "...*Ruth replied, 'Don't urge me to leave you or to turn back from you. Where you go I will go, and where you stay I will stay. Your people will be my people and your God my God.'*"

Here we have an honest example of accepting God's authority. Many accept Jesus as their Savior in death; but recognizing His authority in the here and now, and allowing Him to be your Lord in *this* life, is necessary for full submission to Him.

You may have noticed that Ruth's commitment comes at a time when Naomi is not at all trusting in God, but instead feeling His hand had gone out against her. I find it interesting that Ruth would choose to follow God when her only experience of Him comes through distress. Naomi certainly isn't making what I would call a good statement about Him.

We have looked at Naomi's bitterness, expressed through changing her name to Mara. Ironically, her real name; Naomi means "pleasant." She certainly was anything but pleasant at the time Ruth claimed God as her own! I have wondered, "What brought Ruth to this point, when all she had seen of this God had been through famine and death?"

Ruth's choice tells me that Ruth knew she was dealing with a real and mighty God. Think about it, Ruth *must* have asked herself, "why would Naomi continue to claim a God that she thought was punishing her unless she knew He was the real thing?!"

Ruth's fear of God is evident in what she says about God dealing "ever so severely" with her if anything but death was to separate her from Naomi. Now, whether or not Ruth's fear of God at this time was healthy or not, one thing is for sure – she knew "Who" He was and that He was not to be dismissed! And by the end of her story, God makes sure that Ruth knows also of His mighty love!

God's faithfulness was revealed when Naomi learned that it was the fields of Boaz where Ruth was gleaning.

Ruth 2:3

> *"So she went out, entered a field and began to glean behind the harvesters. As it turned out, she was working in a field belonging to Boaz, who was from the clan of Elimelech."*

[Elimelech being Naomi's deceased husband]

I love that, *"as it turned out"* phrase! That's subtle for *"God at work here!"*

When Naomi finds out, she shouts her reaction.

Ruth 2:20

> *"The LORD bless him!" Naomi said to her*
> *daughter-in-law. "He* [God] *has not stopped showing*
> *His kindness to the living and the dead"*
> *She added, "That man is our close relative; he is one*
> *of our guardian-redeemers."* [my notation]

And the faithfulness of God is again confirmed when Ruth gives birth to Obed and the women of Bethlehem shout praises to the Lord for renewing Naomi's life.

But the book of Ruth holds yet another example of respect for God, and it comes to us a little less obviously. It is through Ruth's recognition of a kinsman redeemer (put simply; "kinsman" meaning a male relative and "redeemer" meaning rescuer).

Here is where we do one of those switches from the literal to the symbolic. Ruth acknowledges Boaz as her kinsman redeemer when the following words are exchanged between Ruth and Boaz.

Ruth3:9

> *"Who are you?' he asked. 'I am your servant Ruth,'*
> *she said. 'Spread the corner of your garment over me, since*
> *you are a kinsman-redeemer.'"* [emphasis added]

Now for Ruth, she was literally speaking of Boaz as both her kin, her relation *and* as her redeemer; not in the spiritual sense, but in the physical and cultural sense. Boaz was redeeming her and her mother-in-law from a life of hardship.

Let's see how the Lord our God is described in His word as our Physical *and* Spiritual Redeemer!

Job 19:25

> *I know that my redeemer lives, and that in the end he will stand on the earth.*

Psalm 78:35

> *They remembered that God was their Rock, that God Most High was their Redeemer.*

Titus 2:13b-14

> *... our great God and Savior, Jesus Christ, [14] who gave himself for us to redeem us from all wickedness and to purify for himself a people that are his very own, eager to do what is good.*

What word (or form of the word) is used in all three verses?

Jesus is our redeemer, but do you know that He is also our kinsman - our kin?!

Jesus describes those who do His Father's will as family.

Matthew 12:50

> *"For whoever does the will of my Father in heaven is my brother and sister and mother."*

And we find this concept of a family repeated in the Book of *Romans.*

Romans 8:16-17

> *"The Spirit himself testifies with our spirit that we are God's children. Now if we are children, then we are heirs—heirs of God and co-heirs with Christ."*

The book of *Ezekiel* offers us a definite link enabling us to make this symbolic connection between Ruth's recognition of Boaz as her kinsman redeemer and our recognition of God – as our redeemer, through Christ.

This is only one of many verses in the retelling of what the Lord told the prophet Ezekiel to express to the people of Jerusalem. It is part of a wonderful metaphor or word picture of the Israelites journey with God.

Ezekiel 16:8

> *"Later I passed by, and when I looked at you and saw that you were old enough for love, I spread the corner of my garment over you and covered your nakedness. I gave you my solemn oath and entered into a covenant with you, declares the Sovereign LORD, and you became mine."'*
>
> [emphasis added]

Sound familiar? Ruth asked Boaz to cover her with a corner of his garment as a sign that he would become her husband, vowing to protect and watch over her.

In a later book in this series I get more into this when exploring Christ as our husband, so forgive me this teaser; but it is especially appropriate that God would complete this example of a virtuous woman he gave us in Ruth with her being wed to her kinsman redeemer.

Just as Ruth is an example of a woman made virtuous in God, Boaz is an example of the kinsman redeemer we have in Christ!

But while Ruth could have had other kinsman redeemers, (in fact we are told in the Book of Ruth that there was another that preceded Boaz in line); there is but One who is able to redeem *us* from our sin and separation from God.

Just as Ruth found someone to rescue and protect her, we have a Lord who will do the same for us.

Our One and Only Kinsman Redeemer - Jesus Christ!

As we finish looking at Ruth as our example of a virtuous woman, I'll share one more metaphorical tie involving garments and our being virtuous in Christ.

The Hebrew word for the garment Boaz draped over Ruth (*Ruth 3:9*) is the same word for the garment God draped over the Israelites (*Ezekiel 16:8*). In the Hebrew definition, this garment is described as… a wing!
(1)

Ruth 2:12

> *"May the LORD repay you for what you have done. May you be richly rewarded by the LORD, the God of Israel, under whose wings you have come to take refuge."*

Have you chosen to seek refuge under the wings of God?

If so, write out your thoughts in a prayer to God.

If not, my prayer for you is that you will continue seeking Him!

Throughout the rest of this study series, we will take a closer look at the description of a virtuous woman, and continue to connect these verses with other passages and books of the Bible. We will look at more women of the Bible who trusted God with their lives and how He blessed them. We are just getting started! I hope you will continue to join me!

Finish chapter six by reading *Zechariah 14:4* aloud.

> *On that day his feet will stand on*
> *the Mount of Olives, east of Jerusalem, and*
> *the Mount of Olives will be split in two from east to*
> *west, forming a great valley, with half of the mountain*
> *moving north and half moving south.*

Just as stated in *Job 19:25* [2], there will come a day when our Lord Jesus will return and His feet will again stand on the Earth. Now is the time to accept Jesus as your Lord *and* Savior, and prepare your heart for His return!

---

[2] *I know that my redeemer lives, and that in the end he will stand on the earth.*

Book One

Review/Discussion Questions for Individual or Group Study:

Introduction:

We've all been given the same commandment. A commandment that tells us to, *"Love the Lord your God with all your heart and with all your soul and with all your mind and with all your strength"* Mark 12:30.

What could this look like in your daily life?

Chapter One:

Romans 3:23-24 says, *"...for all have sinned and fall short of the glory of God, and all are justified freely by his grace through the redemption that came by Christ Jesus."*

Why is this so important for us to know?

Your heavenly Father is so in love with you and He has great desire for you to know and trust Him. So much so, that Jesus gave His life to make sure that was possible!

What are some ways you can start to become *fully acquainted* with God?

Chapter Two:

When we turn away from God, we inevitably turn toward something else, and often that something becomes a replacement for God.

What is it that you often turn to when you are in need of comfort from the stresses of life?

Hebrews 12:1-2b says, "Therefore, since we are surrounded by such a great cloud of witnesses, let us throw off everything that hinders and the sin that so easily entangles, and let us run with perseverance the race marked out for us. ² Let us fix our eyes on Jesus, the author and perfecter of our faith…"

Who are the witnesses in your life? And in what ways can you show them that your eyes are fixed on Jesus?

Chapter Three:

Proverbs 31:26 says of the virtuous woman, *"She speaks with wisdom, and faithful instruction is on her tongue."*

Why do you think a virtuous woman is so careful with her words?

Our being virtuous women is more about our trust in God than anything we could accomplish on our own, or our status in life.

How does this mean to you?

Chapter Four:

Judges 21:25 says, *"In those days Israel had no king; everyone did as they saw fit."* This resulted in a food *and* spiritual famine.

In today's world, many people refuse to follow King Jesus. How has that affected our society?

Sometimes challenges and hardships are brought on by none other than ourselves. We often find ourselves in painful places, through lack of obedience and our need to be in control.

What can we do to avoid this pitfall?

Chapter Five:

Romans 10:9 says, *"If you declare with your mouth, "Jesus is Lord," and believe in your heart that God raised him from the dead, you will be saved."*

Why do you think we are asked to declare with our mouth that "Jesus is Lord" to be saved?

God has promised, *"… He will never leave you or forsake you"* (*Hebrews 13:5*).

How does this truth affect your view of Him? Your relationship with Him?

Chapter Six:

Romans 8:16-17 says, *"The Spirit himself testifies with our spirit that we are God's children. Now if we are children, then we are heirs—heirs of God and co-heirs with Christ."*

What does this tell you about the love that God has for you as His beloved daughter?

Just as Ruth found someone to rescue and protect her, we have a Lord who will do the same for us. *Our One and Only Kinsman Redeemer - Jesus Christ!*

What does *this* tell you about the love that God has for you as His beloved daughter?

Bibliography

1. **Webster, Merriam and.** http://www.merriam-webster.com/. [online]

2. **Strong, James.** *Strong's Exhaustive Concordance.* Tulsa, Oklahoma : American Christian College Press, 1894.

Resources

Bible Gateway - https://www.biblegateway.com/ [online]

Made in the USA
Las Vegas, NV
23 May 2023

72421914R00049